BE AN ECO HERO!

OUTDOORS

Franklin Watts
First published in Great Britain in 2022 by The Watts Publishing Group

Credits
Design and project management: Raspberry Books
Art Direction: Sidonie Beresford-Browne
Designer: Vanessa Mee
Illustrations: Lisa Koesterke

HB ISBN: 978 1 4451 8181 3
PB ISBN: 978 1 4451 8182 0

Printed in China

MIX
Paper from
responsible sources
FSC® C104740

Franklin Watts
An imprint of
Hachette Children's Group
Part of The Watts Publishing Group
Carmelite House
50 Victoria Embankment
London EC4Y 0DZ

An Hachette UK Company
www.hachette.co.uk

www.hachettechildrens.co.uk

BE AN ECO HERO!

OUTDOORS

Florence Urquhart and Lisa Koesterke

W

FRANKLIN WATTS

LONDON·SYDNEY

CONTENTS

Outdoor places 6

Our planet 8

Living things 10

Web of life 12

Plants for life 14

Growing plants 16

Recycling nature 18

Helping wildlife 20

Take litter home 22

Nature spotter 24

Eco hero activities 26

Quiz 28

Glossary 30

Learn more 31

Index 32

OUTDOOR PLACES

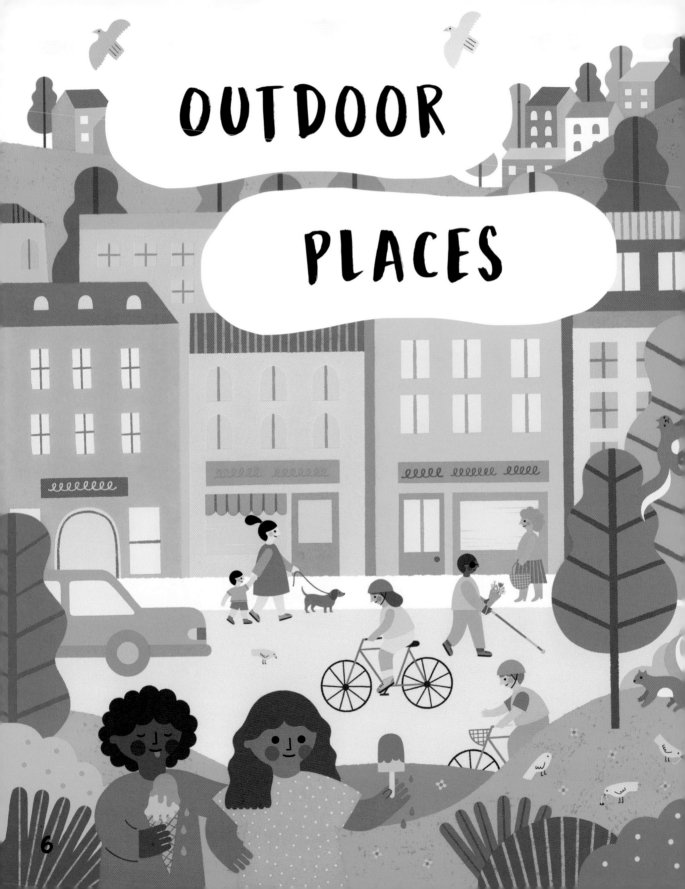

Our homes are in cities, towns and villages. All these places are also homes and habitats to other animals and plants.

Eco heroes look after the environment!

You can be an eco hero by learning about your environment. There is a lot you can do to keep your environment clean and healthy. Looking after habitats helps the animals and plants that live in them.

OUR PLANET

Our environment is the planet we live on.
It has the things we need
to live, such as:

air to breathe

water to drink

soil to grow food.

Our environment also gives us
medicines, fuels and materials
to make things.

The problem is that many of the things
we all do pollute and damage the environment.
Pollution makes the air, soil and water
dirty and unhealthy.

Using less and making less rubbish
cuts down pollution. This is better
for plant and animal habitats.

LIVING
THINGS

You can be an eco hero by learning about living things. Your environment is made up of an amazing mixture of different plant and animal life.

AN ECO HERO KNOWS:

If you pick a leaf or flower, or break a branch, you can harm an animal's habitat or food.

You can learn a lot by watching wildlife.

If you do pick things up, you should put them back where you found them.

I try not to harm any wildlife - even tiny insects!

WEB OF LIFE

Eco heroes know that all animals
and plants are part of a web of life.
All the animals and plants need
each other to live and grow.

Insects are small animals that play
an important part in the web of life.
Bees and butterflies help plants
make their seeds by carrying pollen
from flower to flower.

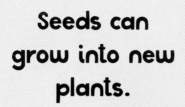

Seeds can grow into new plants.

Some plants need birds and other animals to eat and spread their seeds.

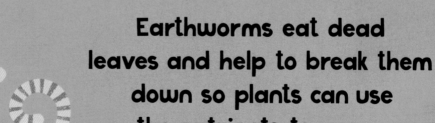

Earthworms eat dead leaves and help to break them down so plants can use the nutrients to grow.

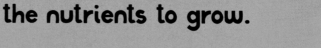

PLANTS FOR LIFE

Trees are the biggest plants. Trees are an important part of the web of life. Animals need trees for food and shelter.

If there were no plants, there would be no air to breathe or food to eat. Trees and other plants make oxygen, which humans and other animals need to breathe.

PLANTS GIVE US:

Fuel

Food to eat

Materials to make things

Oxygen to breathe

and much more!

Eco heroes know we need to look after plants.

GROWING PLANTS

You can be an eco hero by growing plants for flowers and food.

~

Grow plants in pots or window boxes if you don't have a garden.

~

Make sure your plants have plenty of water and sunlight.

Before you recycle or throw away things, see if you can use them for gardening.

Use lollysticks as plant labels.

Lollystick label

Yogurt plant pot

Plastic bottle cloche

There are lots of ways to reuse things in the garden. See if you can find different ways.

RECYCLING NATURE

If you have a garden or yard, you can be an eco hero by making compost from kitchen and garden waste.

Compost is full of nutrients that plants need to grow.

Inside your compost bin, earthworms and other creatures, such as slugs and beetles, eat the waste. They help it to rot and break it down.

Earthworms also keep the rotting material healthy by making holes that let air in and water out.

Compost

It takes about a year for the waste to be broken down into compost. You can add compost to soil to help plants grow.

Don't throw out your apple cores - put them in the compost!

HELPING

WILDLIFE

You can be an eco hero by doing simple things to help wildlife. For example, keeping your cat indoors at night (especially at sunrise and sunset) stops them killing so many mice and birds.

A noisy bell on a cat's collar keeps birds and other small animals safe.

Bell on collar

BE AN ECO HERO BY:

Putting out food and water for birds regularly. If you feed birds, they have more babies. So if you stop putting out food, there may not be enough food for all the birds.

Make sure you put out the right food for wildlife.

Feeding wildlife the wrong food can be very bad for them.

If you put out food for the birds, make sure feeders are high up so cats cannot reach them.

TAKE LITTER

HOME

Take litter home with you to reuse or recycle, or put it in a bin. Make sure you only leave footprints when you go home.

AN ECO HERO KNOWS:

Litter such as metal cans takes many years to break down.

If you throw something in a rubbish bin, it will go to a landfill site and we are running out of room to bury rubbish.

Litter is dangerous for wildlife.

Try to leave places as you found them.

NATURE SPOTTER

We need to learn more about plant and animal habitats. Many animals and plants are dying out because habitats have been destroyed by farming and other human activities.

BE AN ECO HERO BY:

Making a note
of birds and other
animals you have seen
where you live.

Sending your
information to nature
groups who can use
it to help wildlife.

Watch the
birds

Make a
record

Looking out for information
about surveys on TV and on
the Internet.

I found out that newts are in
danger because their habitats
are disappearing!

ECO HERO ACTIVITIES

Here are some more simple ways you can get active to be an eco hero outdoors.

If you have the space, plant your own tree.

Choose a tree that you know is popular with wildlife.

Remember to find out how big a tree will grow before you make your choice.

Or you can choose a tree for its fruit.

Collect pet hair, dead grass, scraps of cotton and pieces of wool.

Stuff it in an old fruit net.

Hang it high in a tree in the spring and watch the birds collect materials to build their nests.

Find out about wildlife organisations close to where you live.

You and your family can help local groups by joining in with clean-up operations at wildlife areas such as ponds and beaches.

QUIZ

1. How do bees and butterflies help plants?

a. They carry pollen from flower to flower
b. They cut their leaves
c. They water them every night

2. What is the biggest type of plant?

a. Grass
b. Trees
c. Nuts

3. What do plants make which helps us breathe?

a. Carbon dioxide
b. Pollen
c. Oxygen

4. What is compost?

a. A kind of bread
b. A soft, brown substance made from rotted plant material
c. A powder made by flowers

5. Which of these creatures would you want to find in a compost pile?

a. Earthworms
b. Puppies
c. Birds

6. What is recycling?

a. Using materials again to make them into something new
b. Riding your bicycle around in circles
c. Using materials once and throwing them away

7. What should you do with your litter when you're outside?

a. Leave it on the ground
b. Take it home or put it in a bin
c. Put it out of the way in a tree

8. Which of these would help birds?

a. Letting a cat out at night
b. Cutting down trees
c. Putting up a birdfeeder

9. What is a habitat?

a. A home for a plant or animal
b. A bag for shopping
c. A funny way of talking

10. What will you do to be an eco hero today?

ANSWERS:

1] a. They carry pollen from flower to flower
2] b. Trees
3] c. Oxygen
4] c. A soft, brown substance made from rotted plant material
5] a. Earthworms
6] a. Using materials again to make them into something new
7] b. Take it home or put it in a bin
8] c. Putting up a birdfeeder
9] a. A home for a plant or animal

What did you score?

1-3:
It would be a good idea to read the book again.

4-6:
You're almost there.

7-10:
You are an ECO HERO!

GLOSSARY

cloche — a glass or plastic cover to keep tiny plants safe and warm.

compost — a soft, brown substance made from rotted plant material. You can make compost in a special bin.

environment — the space around you. It can be a building, a garden, a playground or a busy street. It can even include the whole planet.

fuel — the material used to make heat or light, usually by being burned. Coal, gas and oil are types of fuel.

habitat — a home for a plant or animal.

healthy — to be fit and well.

landfill site — a huge hole in the ground where rubbish is buried.

material — a substance that is used to make things.

nutrient — a substance that plants get from soil that they need to live and grow.

oxygen — a type of gas that animals need to live. A gas is an air-like substance that you cannot see.

pollen — a powder made by flowers.

pollute — to make air or water dirty.

recycle — to use materials again to make them into something new.

rot — to go slimy or mouldy and break down.

seed — the part of a plant from which a new plant can grow.

seedling — a tiny plant that grows from a seed.

web — a net-like structure made of thin threads. If one thread breaks the web falls apart.

LEARN MORE

This book shows you some of the ways you can be an eco hero. But there is plenty more you can do outdoors to save the planet. Here are some websites that can help you learn more:

www.rspb.org.uk/youth
Lots of information about getting involved in campaigns and competitions, plus great games and activities.

www.actionfornature.org
Eco awards, nature friendly information and fun and games.

www.wildlifewatch.org.uk
Discover your local wildlife trust and the activities they run.

www.rspca.org.uk
You can find information about wildlife on this site. Follow links to: Advice and welfare then click on: Wildlife.

www.woodlandtrust.org.uk
The Woodland Trust's blog posts have a section of activities for children and families.

Note to parents and teachers: Every effort has been made by the Publishers to ensure that these websites are suitable for children, that they are of the highest educational value, and that they contain no inappropriate or offensive material. However, because of the nature of the Internet, it is impossible to guarantee that the contents of these sites will not be altered. We strongly advise that Internet access is supervised by a responsible adult.

INDEX

animals 7, 9, 10, 11, 12, 14, 15, 20, 24, 25

birds 13, 17, 20, 21, 25, 27, 31

compost 18, 19, 30

earthworms 13, 19

food 11, 14, 15, 16, 21

fuels 9, 15, 30

gardening 16, 17, 18

habitats 7, 9, 11, 24, 30

insects 11, 12

landfill sites 23, 30

litter 22, 23

materials 9, 15, 27, 30

oxygen 15, 30

plants 7, 9, 10, 11, 12, 13, 14, 15, 16, 17, 18, 19, 24, 30

pollution 9, 30

recycling 18, 22, 30

rubbish 9, 23, 30

seeds 12, 13, 17, 30

trees 14, 15, 26, 27

web of life 12, 13, 14

wildlife 11, 20, 21, 23, 25, 26, 27, 31

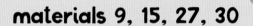